YOUR KNOWLEDGE HAS VALUE

Bibliographic information published by the German National Library:

The German National Library lists this publication in the National Bibliography; detailed bibliographic data are available on the Internet at http://dnb.dnb.de .

Imprint:

Copyright © 2019 GRIN Verlag
Print and binding: Books on Demand GmbH, Norderstedt Germany
ISBN: 9783346090232

This book at GRIN:

https://www.grin.com/document/509902

Ebrima Sowe

The weaknesses of the African Human Rights system in comparison with the Inter-American regional human rights System

GRIN Verlag

GRIN - Your knowledge has value

Since its foundation in 1998, GRIN has specialized in publishing academic texts by students, college teachers and other academics as e-book and printed book. The website www.grin.com is an ideal platform for presenting term papers, final papers, scientific essays, dissertations and specialist books.

Visit us on the internet:

http://www.grin.com/

http://www.facebook.com/grincom

http://www.twitter.com/grin_com

The weaknesses of the African Human Rights system in comparison with the Inter-American regional human rights system

Ebrima Sowe[1]

Abstract

The African Human Rights System is seen by many as a weak mechanism that ought to aim for the promotion and protection of human rights in the region. This could be as a result of various legal, professional and financial incapacities. In essence, the urgent need for adjustment in the African Human Rights system prompts me to end with some possible recommendations in this article taking my point of reference from other regional human rights systems such as the Inter-American human rights system.

Discussed in this paper includes a background of the formation (architecture) and the role of accountability played by the regional human rights system (i.e. the African Human Rights System in particular as it is the topic under discussion).
The article also reveals the functional weaknesses of the regional Human Rights system which includes vague provisions in the African Charter, weak judicial arbitration and State compliance mechanisms.

Recommendations in this article are drawn from the Inter-American Human Rights system which has more effective implementation mechanisms.

Keywords: Complementarity, Clawback clauses, Charter, Treaty, Convention

---

[1] Bachelor of Laws (LLB), The University of The Gambia, 2018.

1. Introduction

Human rights systems in the legal perspective works in three (3) levels which begins with the National or Local level where fundamental human rights are entrenched in the country's Constitution and usually enforceable in the superior courts of a state such as the High Court (as it is the case in the Gambia by virtue of section 37 of the 1997 Constitution of the Gambia; human rights could also be enforced in the Regional level (which aims at strengthening the protection and enjoyment of human rights by taking into account, regional considerations such as shared values, customs, cultures and practices of people in a particular region.

However, they are not created to override the enforcement of human rights at the National level, but they rather operate under the principle of complementarity in relation to taking proceedings to the regional court systems (such as the African Court on Human and Peoples' Rights for the African Charter on Human and Peoples' Rights; the Inter-American Court of Human Rights for the Inter-American Commission on Human Rights, the European Court of Human Rights for the European Convention on Human Rights, etc.) in the event domestic/national courts fail to uphold the law or remedy a violation, which will subsequently make it necessary to seek redress beyond national boundaries after exhausting all the local remedies available or possible. This gives right-holders an alternative or chance to bring their claim before a regional body provided that the country in question is part of the framework of such regional body; and that all national remedies have either been exhausted or deemed inefficient.

Also, human rights operate in the International level (above regional settlements) when the violation is of concern to the general international community; and when we talk about human rights at the international level, we cannot do so without mentioning the United Nation, which is the first created human rights body after the second world war to uphold freedom, justice, peace, stability and harmonization in the world through the recognition of the inherent dignity and the equal and inalienable rights of all members of the human family as stated in the preamble of the Universal declaration of human rights. The adoption of the Universal Declaration of Human Rights by the United Nation General Assembly (on December 10th 1948)[2] gave rise to the creation of such numerous regional human rights systems as explained above.

However, all except one of these regional and international human rights bodies are not going to be discussed herein, as the discussion will be focussed only on the African Human Rights System with reference to the Inter-American Human Rights system for the purpose of topic relevance.

2. Historical Background on Functional Framework

The African Human Rights System was created under the aegis of the African Union, and is the youngest amongst the judicial or quasi-judicial regional human rights systems[3] . Similar to the Inter-American system (as well as the European system), it is composed of two establishments, which are; a Commission and a Court which together forms its supervisory mechanisms. Hence, the African Human Rights system composed of the African Commission on Human and Peoples' Rights and the African Court on Human and Peoples' Right. The commission aims at the promotion and protection of human rights in the 54 member states of the African Union (Morocco makes it 55 after it has rejoined the African Union in June 2017 but is yet to ratify the African Charter)[4] .

The Commission operates by receiving complaints of alleged human rights violations which will be deemed as communications from individual(s), non-governmental organisations, and states provided the conditions laid down in Article 56 of the African Charter on Human and Peoples' Rights are met for it to be admissible. These conditions are that, the authors identity be indicated (even if the author of the communication request anonymity); that the communication is in line with the present charter; that it is not written in a disparaging or insulting language; not exclusively based on news of the mass media; exhausting all local remedies available unless it is obvious (not based on mare assumptions) that the procedure is unduly prolonged, that the commission receive a communication within a reasonable period from the time local remedies are exhausted and that the communication have no link to cases which have been settled by the States involved in accordance with International principles. In essence, it is noteworthy that such communications are limited on the interpretation of the provisions of rights (being violated) in the African Charter,

---

[2] INGANGE-WA-INGANGE Jean Désiré 'THE AFRICAN HUMAN RIGHTS SYSTEM:CHALLENGES AND PROSPECTS' (2010).

[3] http://www.ijrcenter.org/regional/african/#African_Commi ssion_on_Human_and_Peoples8217_Rights .

[4] International Justice Resource Center – ijr center (n 3 above).

which has 68 articles upon its adoption in 1981 (entered into force in 1986) which contains substantive provisions in; civil and political rights, economic, social rights and cultural rights (Articles 15-17), collective and development rights, peoples' rights (19-24), limitations on rights and individual duties as all expressed in such articles of the charter . As a result of the emergence of such rights, it engages in its protective mandate by reviewing reports and communications from state parties on compliance with the African Charter, investigate violations of specific human rights issues and issuing non-binding recommendations to states that they found violating the charter upon reviewing communications from individuals and non-governmental organisations. The African Commission on Human and Peoples' rights hold two (2) ordinary sessions that are frequently held every year; and when circumstances requires it, it may also hold extraordinary sessions upon request by the Chairperson of the Commission or majority of its Commissioners. It is in such sessions that periodic reports submitted by state parties are considered by the African Commission.

Aside from the Commission, the African Human Rights system also has a court that complements the work of the commission in protecting and safeguarding human rights in the region. This is the African Court on Human and Peoples' Rights which came into existence through the Protocol to the African Charter on Human and Peoples' Rights after its adoption by the Organization for African Unity (OAU) in June 1998[5] which later came into force in 2004 after it was ratified by more than 15 countries[6] . This was a dream African governments have since before the 1990s, as they were wary of creating a permanent regional human rights court that could issue legally binding judgements to tackle its weakness in terms of enforcement. However the court have jurisdiction only on those states that have ratified the protocol of the African Court on Human and Peoples' Rights earlier referred to herein. The court, like the Inter-American

Court of Human Rights, has advisory (on the interpretation of the provisions of the charter) and contentious jurisdiction which is suitable for the trials of concrete cases referred to it by the Commission. The African Human Right system (differing from the Inter-American system[7]), provides a mechanism where individuals and non-governmental organisations can directly file cases to the court provided the states concerned signed and ratified the court's optional protocol (i.e. where the state concerned made the necessary declaration under Article 34 of the Court's Protocol to allow these complaints) accepting its contentious jurisdiction thereby enabling it to hear cases directly by individuals and NGOs. The declaration being referred to is highlighted in the provision of Article 34(6) as quoted below:

At the time of the ratification of this Protocol or any time thereafter, the State shall make a declaration   accepting the competence of the court to receive cases under article 5(3) of this protocol. The Court shall not receive any petition under article 5(3) involving a State Party which has not made such a declaration.

Also article 5(3) of the protocol states that; *'The Court may entitle relevant NGOs ... and individuals to institute cases directly before it, in accordance with article 34(6) of this Protocol.'*

This Protocol suggests a more effective regional human right system.

However, the mere addition of this court in the African Human Rights system, although being a significant development for the promotion of human rights in the region, it is unlikely by itself to address the weaknesses the African Human Rights system is facing in the promotion of human rights in the region since its inception. These issues (as well as recommendations in reference to the Inter-American system) are further discussed in the paragraphs below.

---

[5] Protocol to the African Charter on Human and Peoples' Rights on the Establishment of an African Court on Human and Peoples' Rights, Assembly of Heads of State and Government of the Organization of African Unity, Ougadougou, Burkina Faso, June 1998, OAU/LEG/MIN/AFCHPR/PROT.(1) Rev.2. [accessed from https://www.brooklaw.edu/~/media/EF2EEF78190940C49D E0937537CD946B.pdf

[6] This is why the proposed merger of the African Court of Justice and Human Rights (with the African Court on Human and Peoples' Rights) is still yet to materialize, as only 5 countries have ratified the protocol as of now, out of the 15 needed ratifications for it to enter into force.

[7] In the Inter-American system, Only States Parties to the American Convention and the Inter-American Commission on Human Rights have the power to appear before the Court .>>http://www.corteidh.or.cr/tablas/r33140.pdf

3. Weaknesses of the System [with recommendations]

Deducing from the above paragraph, it could be understood that the African Human Rights System is weakened by certain factors which makes it fall short of being an effective mechanism for the protection and promotion of human rights in the region due to its structural formation and limited functioning especially with regards to its less noticed accountability role in addressing human rights violations by its member states.

❖ One of these shortcomings is caused by the 'clawback' clauses and vague provisions with regards to enforcing certain rights. These are clauses that offer certain rights, at the same time limit such rights by using certain terms in the provision such as where a provision is made and then followed or preceded by 'except for reasons and conditions previously laid down by law', 'subject to law and order', 'within the law', 'abides by the law', as well as other forms of justification for the 'protection of National Security' among other restrictions[8] , that enable countries with draconian laws (most of which were in place since colonialism and hence not familiar to the young African human rights system of the Charter) to use it as an opportunity to restrict the basic human rights of its citizens to the extent allowed by domestic law without fearing accountability for such violations on the justification of such clawback clauses that the African regional instrument (African Charter) provides.

Also, the vagueness in the definition or lack of clear indication on derogatory clauses and the binding nature of the African Court and Commission's decisions have provided room for State parties to neglect their duty of submitting reports of their human rights activities to the Commission as required under Article 62. For example, with regards to right of every human being to life, as provided for in the Charter, the Charter recognizes this right but the vagueness of the definition of the concept of 'human being' has left loop holes for each State and individuals as well who will determine its meaning based on their individual understandings. Such inconsistency prompts scholars like Murray to suggest that, definitions in the Charter should include concepts and terms that would prevent extra judicial killings (by States and Individuals)[9]. These problems leading to an ineffective human rights system could be remedied by conducting a revision of the Charter, and delete or incorporate alongside such clawback clauses explicit provisions on non-derogable rights, as well as insert other provisions that specify which rights states can derogate from, when, and 'under what circumstances' which is put in quote because it seems to be settled by the Charter on its provision that notice should be given to the Commission as stipulated in Article 58 of the African Charter.

Recommendation:

The African Charter should adopt the approach of the Inter-American human rights system in dealing with this matter; as the Inter-American human rights system through the Inter-American Convention on Human Rights (formally adopted in 1969 and entered into force in July 1978[10] - thus older than the African Charter.) explicitly lays out a fundamental set of obligations which unambiguously defines how states are required to treat their own citizens . This is a lacking essential in the African Human rights system (which raise controversial issues on its language of duties, wherein it express the view that individual rights cannot make sense in a social and political vacuum hence listing the duties in relation to the state, community/family, other individuals among others without stating the mechanisms or what amounts to the breach of such duties, and as well seeking to balance the rights of the individual with those of the state or community through the imposition of such duties on individuals, thereby contemplating the two types of duties, which is duty of the individual to the state and the other way round) instead of dedicating more focus on the State's responsibility in protecting the human rights of its subjects. This is the advantage of the American Convention over the African Charter, as it does not only regulate the behaviour of states towards one another but also the conduct of states towards individuals in such states[11].

---

[8] As found in Articles 133-137 of the African Charter on Human and Peoples' Rights.

[9] Murray R, 'developments in the African human rights system 2003-04', (2006) 6/1 Human Rights Law review, p. 169

[10] American Convention on Human Rights, O.A.S.Treaty Series No. 36, 1144 U.N.T.S. <<accessed via http://www.corteidh.or.cr/tablas/r33140.pdf >>.

[11] Article 4(1) of the Inter-American Convention on Human Rights.

Also as earlier mentioned, the African Charter does not have a general derogation clause which itself accords room for the use of such clawback clauses by States to suspend or strictly restrict many fundamental rights in their domestic laws without set out derogation clauses for certain fundamental human rights. In comparison with the Inter-American human right system, the Inter-American Convention on Human Rights though technically, is not a treaty that is legally binding, it is still considered by the Inter-American Court of Human Rights and the Inter-American Commission on human rights as a credible source of human rights provisions that member states must abide by. As a matter of fact and law, many earlier human rights instruments such as the Universal Declaration of Human Rights are so reflected in the American Convention on Human Rights, it becomes binding in the sense that States under the American Human Rights system, commit 'to respect the rights and freedoms recognized' in the Convention as stipulated in Article 1 of the American Convention. As a result, their Convention thus becomes a formally binding legal document through which States pledge to one another a minimum standard of treatment for all individuals within their jurisdiction. These obligations were possible by States under the Convention taking further measures by committing themselves to enacting any domestic legislation that may be necessary to give effect to these rights and freedoms[12], as oppose to the African system, where the Charter give States the room to make reservations for certain provisions or protocols, hence limiting the enforcement of rights by drawback clauses which renders the Charters role in promoting and protecting human rights in the region unenforceable and pointless of its purpose of creation. These issues are coupled with the incompatibility of the domestic laws of member States of the African human rights system with the African Charter which can be said to be caused by the existence of such laws before the creation of the African Charter, thus having less regard with regards to consistency (especially with the many clawback clauses in the Charter) in the provisions of the two set of documents. A clear example of the occurrence of such can be seen in the case of **Tanganyika Law Society & Another v Tanzania**[13] where amendments to the Tanzanian Constitution (domestic law) violated the rights of the citizens accorded by the African Charter, hence an issue of incompatibility of domestic and regional legislation. Eventhough the African Court in its decision highlighted on the obligation to cure the incompatibility found in domestic laws, this can be viewed as an obligation limited to Tanzania, except and until it is incorporated as a binding legislation in the Charter. Thus, this could be fixed by taking reference from the Inter-American system approach as discussed herein, in revising legislations, and by inserting provisions in the Charter that will expressly state that all states in the African Charter should take it as an obligation to see to it that the human rights provision in the Charter are binding (as in the American system) and incorporated in their laws as entrenched clauses or provisions injected into the Charter that will strictly emphasize on the compatibility of domestic laws and the removal of clawback clauses or derogation clauses that will strictly narrow down the use of certain clawback clauses such as the derogation of rights due to public danger or emergency situation, to defined circumstances, as eminent in the American Convention. This for example, is provided for in Article 27 of the American Convention that such derogation is only allowed provided that they do not involve 'discrimination on the ground of race, colour, sex, language, religion or social origin'.

❖ Moreover, the African human right system is weak in function in a way that, unlike its counterpart (the Inter-American system), the African Charter is less active in the judicial arbitration mechanism with strict enforcement procedures. It rather focussed on the diplomatic settlement of dispute, and thus place less emphasis on the use of judicial arbitration (as the African Commission is more reluctant in referring cases to the African Court in events State parties fail to abide by its recommendations) as put forward by Makau Mutua[14]. In fact, this is logical in the sense that though the African Court exists, it is not an initiative that was called for by the Charter (but was rather establish by a Protocol), as the provisions do not even reflect on it unlike the Inter-American human rights Convention or other regional human right instruments. This shows its preference on diplomatic settlement (which is ineffective especially in the African setting where most African heads especially those that overstay in power, tend to care less about diplomacy in the face of their sporadic behaviour to compliance with International law such as the African Charter. An example of such is the neglect or reluctance by State parties to comply with Article 62 of the African Charter, which obliges them to submit regular reports to the African Commission on the status of

---

[12] The Inter-American Convention (n 13 above) at Article 2.

[13] App. No. 011/2011 – Rev. Christopher R. Mtikila v. United Republic of Tanzania.

[14] Mutua M, 'The African human rights system: A critical Evaluation', (2005), p. 20.

human rights protection in their jurisdictions; but because the Charter does not clarify its binding nature towards this regard, States as well do as they choose (which they often do except for the obligations found in the universal human rights instruments (beyond regional), which indicates their binding character explicitly.

Recommendation:

In connection to the problem mentioned above, the ineffective problem of the African human rights system and the clash of roles or duties could be linked to the approach of vesting both the promotional and protective roles of the human rights system all on the African Commission instead of vesting the exclusive promotional role on the African Commission which has been the centrepiece of its operation[15] although the Commissions mandate includes the protective function of State reporting and the consideration of communication (which can all be transferred to the Court's mandate, and as well encourage parties to the African Charter to make the declaration in the Court's Protocol); and protective function wholly on the African Court instead of proposing for the creation of a new African court that will do the same mistake of taking the double function of the Commission and the court without abolishing the Commission (which will leave it even more dormant if that should materialise). So long as this is not reviewed and restructured, and preference taken in the Inter-American context of making provisions formally binding on its members, both the African Commission and the Court will continue to be a disappointment in the existence of the African regional human rights system.

Furthermore, the OAU Charter (i.e. the African Charter) have been criticized for not expressly referring to the concept of human rights or its protection but rather making it a secondary objective alongside its primary objective of uniting independent African States instead[16] (i.e. doing away with Colonialism); when the Inter-American Convention is being viewed primarily by its members as a reflection of a source of law that takes the form of a formally binding document with focused on its human rights provisions.

In relation to this, I totally agree with Judge Kebba Mbaye on his opinion that, the pursuit of political stability and development in Africa at this time was put forth before the protection of human rights[17], hence diverting or dividing its focus and attention on the promotion and protection of human rights in the region, hence contributing to its weak nature.

Most importantly too the African human rights system lack an effective mechanism in place that will force States to comply with binding decisions from the African Court on human and Peoples' Rights which is the highest authority in the region that should monitor or regulate States' compliance with its final decisions that are binding. However, it is rather unfortunate that the execution of judgements by the States is obligatory but voluntary by virtue of Article 30 of the Court's Protocol[18]. Hence implying that States cannot be necessarily force to comply. The Protocol sees that notifying the Commission, Assembly, African Union, as well as NGOs acts as an important mean of pressurizing the condemned States and hence there is no need to force States to comply. This however does not seem to be very effective compared to the Inter-American approach of dealing with State compliance to the regional court's decision which are final and binding. The Inter-American Court supervises State compliance[19] instead of the Commission (as in the African system). This is done through ad hoc judgement, assessing whether a state has complied with the remedial measures imposed upon it by the Court. Thus, the Inter-American Court (not the Commission) has taken upon its shoulders the need to guide States further on compliance strategies. The Court may even require further information from other sources (this could be through the request of expert opinions or report) regarding the case in order to evaluate State compliance[20]. The Commission performs the observation duty. In case of a finding of non-enforcement or compliance,

---

[15] Mutua M, 'The African human rights system: A critical Evaluation' at p. 26.

[16] Mangu AMB, (2005) 'The changing human rights landscape in Africa: Organization of African Unity, African Union, New Partner for Africa's Development and the African Court', Netherlands Quarterly of Human Rights, pp. 379-381.

[17] Mbaye K & Ndiaye B, 'The organization of African Unity' in Vasak & Alston P (eds), The International dimensions of Human Rights, (1982), 2 pp. 583-593.

[18] Protocol to the African Charter on Human and Peoples' Rights on the Establishment of an African Court on Human and Peoples' Rights (n 7 above).

[19] Article 65 of the American Convention (n 12 above).

[20]Article 69 (2) of the Rules of Procedure of the Inter-American Court.

additional obligations may be imposed upon such State in order to ensure compliance[21].

Deductively, it could be seen from the above that the American Court goes the extra mile to account for and monitor State compliance rather than merely basing it on threats and presumptions which is less effective, and thus is recommended for the African human rights system to adopt this approach in remedy of its weak mechanisms in dealing with such problem.

4. Conclusion

In conclusion, the African human rights system though being the youngest of the regional human rights system is well structured in terms of its formation and composition (as it combines all the generation of rights that its counterparts accord in different instruments, all in the African Charter). However, it remains the most ineffective mechanism for the enforcement of human rights due to its weak enforcement mechanisms caused by certain factors which makes it fall short of its mandate in promoting and protecting human rights in the region as discussed in this paper alongside the Inter-American system which though also had its setbacks, is better off in existence. Ultimately, I believe the African Human Rights system, with its excellent formation can conform into an effective regional human rights enforcement with the adoption of its predecessor counterparts' (especially the Inter-American human rights system) enforcement mechanism and curing the defects associated with the enforcement system such as the clawback clauses, among others as discussed above; by thoroughly revising both the Charter and the institutions especially the African Court, which was not even presumed by the drafters of the African Charter on human and Peoples' Rights.

These adjustments I believe will go a long way in restoring the confidence of the people in the enforcement of their human rights using the regional human rights bloc unhesitatingly in the event the domestic system proves ineffective.

Acknowledgements

This is my first article on the subject of Human Rights, as a result, I have consulted various sources. Therefore, I must acknowledge that all referenced materials herein were consulted during my research.

References

[1] African (Banjul) Charter on Human and Peoples' Rights, (Adopted 27 June 1981, OAU Doc. CAB/LEG/67/3 rev. 5, 21 I.L.M. 58 (1982), entered into force 21 October 1986) {"http:www.achpr.org/instruments/achpr/" }

[2] Burke-White W, 'Human Rights in the Inter-American System' International Studies Journal / No. 2 / 33

[3] Enabulele AO, „Incompatibility of national law with the African Charter on Human and Peoples" Rights: Does the African Court on Human and Peoples" Rights have the final say?" (2016) 16 African Human Rights Law Journal 1-28 http://dx.doi.org/10.17159/1996-2096/2016/v16n1a1

[4] Mutua M, (2005 Mutua M, (2005) 'The African Human Rights System: A Critical Evaluation'. http://hdr.undp.org/sites/default/files/mutua.pdf

[5] The Constitution of the Republic of The Gambia, 1997 [accessed from http://hrlibrary.umn.edu/research/gambia-constitution.pdf]

---

[21] Rules of Procedure of the Inter-American Court (n 23 above).

YOUR KNOWLEDGE HAS VALUE

- We will publish your bachelor's and
  master's thesis, essays and papers

- Your own eBook and book -
  sold worldwide in all relevant shops

- Earn money with each sale

Upload your text at www.GRIN.com
and publish for free